# Spaces, Shapes, and Sizes

# Spaces, Shapes, and Sizes

by Jane Jonas Srivastava
Illustrated by Loretta Lustig

Thomas Y. Crowell · New York

LIBRARY OF CONGRESS CATALOGING IN PUBLICATION DATA
Srivastava, Jane Jonas.
    Spaces, shapes, and sizes.
    SUMMARY: Explains in simple terms the concept
of volume.
    1. Volume (Cubic content)—Juvenile literature.
[1. Volume (Cubic content)   2. Weights and
measures] I. Lustig, Loretta. II. Title.
QC104.S64     1980      530′.8      78-22516
ISBN 0-690-03961-1
ISBN 0-690-03962-X lib. bdg.

1   2   3   4   5   6   7   8   9   10
First Edition

# Spaces, Shapes, and Sizes

Stand up.

Stretch your arms and legs out as far as you can.

Sit down on the floor.

Curl yourself into a tight ball.

Every time you move, you change your shape. Your VOLUME stays the same. You take up the same amount of space, no matter what shape you make your body.

The only time the volume of your body changes is when you grow taller or wider, or when you lose weight because you have been sick or you have been on a diet.

If you cut up peeled potatoes to make French fries,
you change their shape. Do you change their total
volume?

If your mother buys yarn for a sweater, the shape of the yarn changes as it is knitted in to the sweater, but its volume stays the same.

Can you think of other things that keep their volume when their shape is changed?

What about the clay you use in your classroom?

What about the sand you play with in your sandbox?

Find a small box. Fill the box with sand. Put a large piece of paper on a table and pour the sand from the box onto the paper. First the sand was in a box shape. Now it is in a cone shape. Has the volume of the sand changed?

Spread the sand out into a flat shape. Spread it into another, different flat shape. Has the volume changed?

Now put the sand back into the box. (A funnel may help you to do this without spilling too much sand.) If you are very careful to put every bit of sand back into the box, the box will be full of sand again. You poured and spread the sand into different shapes, but it kept the same volume. It still takes up the same space—all the space in the box.

13

Look around you. Everything you see takes up space. Everything you see has volume.

Building blocks have volume.

Find 6 blocks that are as wide as they are long as they are high. These blocks are called cubes. At school you may have inch cubes or centimeter cubes. At home you may have some alphabet blocks that are cubes. If you cannot find any cubes to use, you can make some cubes out of cardboard by tracing this pattern.

Fold on the dotted lines and tape the edges together.

Use your cubes to make buildings of different shapes.
Take 4 cubes and put them together in any way you like.
You may have put your 4 cubes together like this

or like this

or like this.

Each building looks different. Is the volume of each
building different?

This building was made with 3 cubes. It has a volume of 3 cubes.

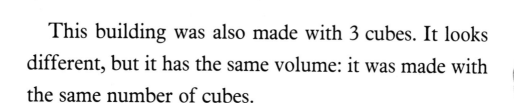

This building was also made with 3 cubes. It looks different, but it has the same volume: it was made with the same number of cubes.

What is the volume of this building?

Make more buildings with a volume of 6 cubes.
Make each building a different shape.

Did you make this building?

This building?

Cubes and buildings have volume. Boxes have volume, too. A box keeps the same volume whether it is empty or full. A box keeps the same volume no matter what is inside it.

Take the box you filled with sand. You can put other things in that box: marbles, crayons, blocks, apples—whatever you choose. Try to guess how many of each thing will fit in the box before you begin to fill it. When it is full, dump it out and count the number of things you used to fill the box.

Perhaps you were able to pack 31 marbles in the box.
Perhaps you were able to pack 17 crayons in the box.
Perhaps you could fit only 2 apples in the box.

Whether the box was filled with 31 marbles or 17 crayons or only 2 apples, it stayed the same size. It probably stayed the same shape, too. The volume of the box stayed the same, no matter what you put into it.

Boxes come in different shapes and sizes, packed with many different things. In your classroom you may find boxes of chalk, boxes of pencils, boxes of crayons. In your home you may find boxes of toothpicks, boxes of cereal, boxes of Band-Aids. The next time you go shopping, look in the stores you visit to find boxes of different shapes and sizes, packed with different things.

Some boxes have a small volume; some boxes have a large volume. Boxes usually have almost the same volume as the things that are packed inside. Otherwise,

if the box is too small, the right number of things will
not fit into it. If the box is too large, the things inside
will rattle around too much.

Suppose you want to take 4 health-food squares to the playground for a snack at recess time. Can you find a box that is just the right size?

Suppose you want to take some snap-together blocks to a friend's house. Can you find a box that has about the same volume as the pieces you want to take?

Boxes with the same shape may have different volumes. Cereal boxes may have the same shape but come in different sizes. Boxes of toothpaste also come in the same shape in several sizes. It is usually easy to tell which box of cereal or toothpaste has the largest volume just by looking at the boxes.

Boxes with different shapes may have the same volume. It is harder to compare the volumes of boxes that have different shapes just by looking at them. Here is a way to compare the volumes of boxes that are different shapes:

Collect a shoe box, a tissue box, a paper-clip box, a toothpick box, and a toothpaste box.

31

Make a big bowl of popcorn and fill each box with popcorn. Count the number of pieces of popcorn it takes to fill each box. (Before you dump the popcorn out of a box to count it, close the box and shake it gently. Open the box. Can you fit any more popcorn into the box?) The box that held the largest number of pieces of popcorn has the largest volume. The box that held the smallest number of pieces of popcorn has the smallest volume. If two boxes held the same amount of popcorn, they have the same volume, even though the boxes may be different shapes.

You have volume; blocks have volume; boxes have volume. Things you put in a box have volume even when they are not in a box. (Remember the experiment you did with sand on pages 4-7.)

Collect a golf ball, a small metal car, a lump of clay, and a small potato. How can you compare the volumes of these things? You can't fill them with popcorn because they are solid! Instead, you can use a jar of water and some crayons to find out which of these things has the greatest volume, which has the smallest volume, and which are between the smallest and the largest volumes.

Find a jar with a top that is wider than the largest thing you have collected. Fill the jar about half full of water, and mark the water level on the outside of the jar with a black crayon. The black crayon mark shows the volume of the water in the jar.

Put the thing that you think has the largest volume into the jar. Perhaps it is the potato. Does the water cover the potato? If not, take out the potato, add more water to the jar, and mark the new water level. (Don't forget to rub off the first black crayon mark.)

Put the potato back into the jar. Mark the new water level with a brown crayon. The brown crayon mark shows the volume of the water *and* the potato.

Take the potato out of the jar, being careful not to spill any water. Put the potato and the brown crayon next to each other on your desk, so you will remember that the brown mark shows the level of the water when the potato is in the jar.

Now put the thing which you think has the next largest volume into the jar. Perhaps it is the lump of clay. Mark the new water level with a red crayon. The red crayon mark shows the volume of the water and the lump of clay.

Take the lump of clay out of the jar and put it next to the red crayon.

Now put the golf ball or the metal car into the jar. Don't forget to mark the water level again, using a crayon of a different color.

Do the same with the last thing you want to compare.

When you have finished, the side of the jar may look like this:

The black mark is lowest on the jar. It shows how much space in the jar was taken up by water alone. Each of the things you put into the jar took up space and made the water level rise. The thing with the largest volume took up the most space, and its mark will be highest on the side of the jar. The mark for the thing with the smallest volume will be closest to the black mark.

Would you like to have an egg for lunch? Would you like to have it boiled, or fried, or scrambled? No matter how the egg is cooked, its volume will be the same. It will take up the same amount of space, though its shape

may be different. It will have the same volume whether you eat it out of the shell or spread it out on a plate.

If you are very hungry, you can ask for an extra-large egg; it will have a larger volume.

Have a good lunch!

## About the Author

Jane Jonas Srivastava has been an elementary school-teacher and has worked on several mathematics curriculum projects. She currently works at home, taking care of her children, Sanjay and Sonia, writing more books, and housekeeping.

Ms. Srivastava graduated from Swarthmore College and received a master's degree in Elementary Education from Harvard University. Her husband is a professor of Biological Sciences at Simon Fraser University. They live in West Vancouver, British Columbia.

## About the Artist

Loretta Lustig graduated from Pratt Institute and has illustrated children's books on a variety of subjects. She has also worked as an art director for several advertising agencies. Ms. Lustig, who enjoys making and collecting odd things, lives in Brooklyn, New York, which she has found to be the ideal place.